# WIDOW-BURNING

# WIDOW-BURNING:

## A NARRATIVE.

BY

HENRY JEFFREYS BUSHBY

GYAN

*Published by*

GYAN

Gyan Publishing House
5, Ansari Road
Daryaganj, New Delhi-110002
Phone: 011-47034999, 9811692060
E-mail: books@gyanbooks.com

*Distribution Network*
gyanbooks.com
India, USA, Canada, UK, Australia



ISBN: 978-93-6433-123-4 (HB)
First Published, 1855

2nd Impression 2024

*Printed at:* Gyan Press, Delhi.



**WIDOW-BURNING**
Author: HENRY JEFFREYS BUSHBY

# WIDOW-BURNING.

*By the same Author.*

**A MONTH in the CAMP before SEBASTOPOL.**
By a NON-COMBATANT. Third Edition. Post 8vo. 5s.

---

LONDON: LONGMAN, BROWN, GREEN, AND LONGMANS.

# WIDOW-BURNING:

## A NARRATIVE.

BY

HENRY JEFFREYS BUSHBY,

OF THE INNER TEMPLE, ESQ., BARRISTER-AT-LAW; LATE OF THE HON. E. I. CO.'S CIVIL SERVICE.

LONDON:
LONGMAN, BROWN, GREEN, AND LONGMANS.
1855.

# WIDOW-BURNING.

On the 30th of August, 1838, the princely city of Oodypore was the scene of a terrible solemnity. About mid-day, a prolonged discharge of artillery from the fort announced the unexpected decease of Maharána Juwán Singh; and, as is usual in tropical climates, preparations for his obsequies immediately commenced. The palace-gate was thronged with the expectant populace. Something, however, in the excitement of their voices and gestures, boded the approach of a spectacle more thrilling than mere pomp could render even a royal funeral. It was not the dead alone whom the eager crowd were waiting to see pass from among them. Sculptured in startling abundance on the tombs of their rulers, the well-known effigies of *women's feet** gave ghastly assurance, that a prince of Oodypore would not that day be gathered to his fathers without a wife, or a concubine, sharing his pyre. The only question was—how many? It was known that the youngest of the two queens came of a family in which the rite was rarely practised; while the suddenness of the Maharána's death had given but scanty time for any of his inferior women to mature so tremendous a resolution. Great, therefore, was the admiration of the multitude when they learnt that, immediately on the fatal tidings reaching the zenána, both the queens and six, out of seven, concubines had determined to burn. The seventh, a favourite, had excused herself on the plea—which, characteristically enough, was at once admitted—that "she felt none of the inspiration deemed necessary to the sanctity of the sacrifice."

It next became the duty of the chief nobles to address the ladies with the forms of dissua-

* The distinctive memorial of a Suttee. The feet of each victim are represented in relief, with the soles outwards, on the face of the mausoleum.

sion. But to these they quickly put an end by an act that rendered retreat impossible:—loosening their hair, and unveiling their faces, they went to the gate of the zenána, and presented themselves before the assembled populace. All opposition to their wishes now ceased. They were regarded as sacred to the departed monarch. Devout ejaculations poured incessantly from their lips. Their movements became invested with a mysterious significance; and their words were treasured up as prophetic.

Meantime the pile had been prepared. The eight victims, dressed in their richest attire, and mounted on horseback, moved with the procession to the cemetery. There they stripped off their ornaments and jewels, distributed gifts to the bystanders, and, lastly, mounting the pile, took their places beside the corpse. As the Maharána had left no son, his nephew, the present Sovereign, applied the torch. The crash of music, the chanting of the priests, and the cries of the multitude arose simultaneously, and the tragedy was consummated. "The father of one of the queens" (concludes the native report) "was present

A 4

during the whole. He is here immersed in contemplation and grief, and his companions are comforting him."

Perhaps, at this point, some of our readers may feel puzzled by the recollection, that Lord William Bentinck is celebrated in numberless works as having put down all atrocities of this kind more than twenty years ago. And true it is that he did so as far as his authority extended; but within that limit the operation was necessarily confined. In other words, out of about 77 millions of souls, this prohibition reached directly only the 37 millions who were British subjects; indirectly, perhaps about 19 millions more, consisting of the subjects of native princes in whose internal management we had some voice; while there remained not less than 21 millions, the subjects of states which, though our allies, could in no degree be reached by the legislation of 1829. The kingdom of Oodypore, or Meywar, was of the last class. The only notice, therefore, that the Governor-General of 1838 (Lord Auckland) could take of the horrors above detailed, was by way of private communication. The Resident at Oodypore was instructed to explain *unofficially* the displeasure with which the British Government had heard of the tragedy, and of the prominent part in it played by the new Sovereign himself. The Resident's opinion was, at the same time, asked as to the most suitable compliment to be paid to those nobles who had sought to dissuade the ladies from their resolution; and the answer was noteworthy. Lord Auckland was apprised, that the personages in question would simply feel "disgraced" by any tribute which should imply that their dissuasions had been meant for aught but decorous forms!

Such was the veneration in which, up to a date so recent, the sacrifice of Suttee was held by a vast proportion of our allies, and such the acquiescence with which the British Government perforce regarded its celebration. Within the last seven years*, however, the rite has occasioned one of the most remarkable movements recorded in Eastern annals. Never before, within historical memory, had the Hindoos exhibited the phenomenon of *religious change*. During that brief period, an agitation has sprung up, which

* Written in September, 1851.

has led more than half the great independent states to repudiate a sacrifice regarded by their forefathers, not only as sacred, but as a standing miracle in attestation of their faith. So extraordinary an exception to the inveterate tyranny of tradition would demand investigation, were it only as a psychological problem; but how much more is this the case when the wonder is known to be the work of a single British officer! We owe to the late lamented Chairman of the Court of Directors* the means of presenting our readers with the first authentic account of this triumph of individual skill and energy.

Strange to say, the movement originated in the very stronghold of the rite. Among the states who gloried in the readiness of their women to brave this supreme test of conjugal devotion, none exercise a wider influence over Hindoo opinion than the small knot of Powers on the north-west frontier, who occupy the provinces known collectively as Rajpootána. The respect paid throughout India to the blood of the Rajpoots—*Anglicè*, "the progeny of princes"—is well known. Matri-

* Major-General Sir Archibald Galloway, K.C.B.

monial alliances with their chiefs are eagerly sought by potentates of thrice their territorial importance. A race of soldiers and hunters, their figures and faces are eminently handsome and martial; their voices loud; and when they laugh, it is with a hearty burst, like Europeans—in broad contrast to the stealthy chuckle of the Bengálee, or to the silent smile of the reserved Mussulman. Unlike those, too, they scorn the pursuits of the desk; and even agriculture has only become common among them since the tranquillisation of the frontier has diminished their opportunities of obtaining military service among their feudal lords. Whatever a Hindoo knows of chivalry or nationality, he deems to be exemplified in this model race. Since, therefore, Rajpoots were renowned for the frequency of their Suttees, the great independent states thought it beneath their orthodoxy to return any other answer to the remonstrances of the British Government against the rite, than that "it would be time enough for them to prohibit it, when Rajpootána led the way."

This they, doubtless, thought, was to postpone the change indefinitely. Many, in truth, and pitiful, were the instances, which seemed to forbid the hope, that Rajpoots would ever consent to take the lead in such a course. One of these has already been given. A second—the last with which we shall pain our readers—must be added, because it illustrates the chief difficulty with which the friends of abolition had to contend. It was the belief of those officers who had acquired the longest experience in Rajpoot affairs, that every attempt on the part of the British Government to remonstrate against Suttee, had been followed by an increase in the number of the sacrifices. This opinion—which, whether right or wrong, naturally carried weight with the Government, and had caused the discouragement of any active interference in the matter—was supposed to receive a further corroboration in the occurrence we are about to narrate.

Early in 1840, the Political Agent, or chargé d'affaires, at the Rajpoot court of Kotah had ventured, on his own responsibility, to break through the cautious reserve thus prescribed, by apprising the chief of that state, that the British Government would be greatly gratified to hear that his Highness had abolished Suttee throughout his dominions. "My friend," replied the prince, "the customs alluded to have been handed down from the first fathers of mankind. They have obtained in every nation of India, and more especially in Rajpootána; for whenever a sovereign of these states has bidden farewell to life, the queens, through the yearnings of the inward spirit, have become Suttees*, notwithstanding that the relatives were averse to the sacrifice, and would fain have prevented it altogether. It is not in the power of a mortal to nullify a divine, though mysterious, ordinance!" With true Oriental complaisance, however, his Highness proceeded to promise his best efforts to undertake the impossibility. "Since"—he concludes,—"it will afford the English Government peculiar pleasure, I shall take such measures as lie in my power to prohibit the practice." It

* "The term Suttee, or Sati, is strictly applicable to the person, not the rite; meaning a pure and virtuous woman; and designates the wife who completes a life of uninterrupted conjugal happiness by the act of Saha-gamana, accompanying her husband's corpse. It has come in common usage to denote the act." —Wilson's *History of British India*, vol. iii. p. 265; where may also be found a lucid and succinct account of the measures taken by Lord W. Bentinck to put down the rite within our own dominions.

appears that nobody, except the officer to whom it was addressed, attached any value to this plausible assurance. The veteran diplomatist who at that time superintended our relations with the Rajpoot States, was even led to augur from it some fresh outbreak of religious zeal in favour of the rite.

An example was not long wanting. About three P.M. on the 29th October, 1840, a Brahmin, by name Luchmun, died at Kotah, and his widow declared her intention of burning with the corpse. The permission of the reigning prince had, in the first instance, to be obtained. Now, therefore, was the time for testing the value of the pledge which he had given to the chargé d'affaires. His Highness absolutely declined to use his authority. The chief constable was, indeed, sent to address the ordinary dissuasions to the woman, and to promise her a livelihood in case she survived; but the victim, as usual, was resolute. To the offer of a maintenance she is reported to have answered:—"There are a hundred people related to me; and I have no such thoughts to annoy me. I am about to obey the influence of God." The sight of her infant son did not shake her. All the marvels which the arts of the priesthood conjure up on such occasions, were employed to convince the populace that it was the will of Heaven that the sacrifice should proceed. "It has been usual"—naïvely wrote the Kotah minister in his exculpatory account of the catastrophe to the chargé d'affaires—"it has been usual, on a disposition to burn being evinced, to confine the individual in a room under lock and key; and, if these efforts should be frustrated by the voluntary bursting of the locks and doors, it was a sure sign that her intention was pure and sincere, and that it was useless to oppose it. *This test was applied on the present occasion, and both locks and doors flew open!* Moreover, it was known that a *Suttee's words, for good or for evil, would assuredly come true;* which of itself deterred any spectator from interfering. Your Agency messenger brought her to the palace, and took her by the hand; though, as she was regarded as dead to the world and all its creatures, this ought not to have been done. He was told to take a guard, and dissuade her if he could, but he did not succeed."

The chief constable soon obtained sufficient warranty of the strength of the woman's determination to satisfy him of the propriety of ordering the pile. Twenty pounds of sandal-wood, and twenty more of cotton rope, together with faggots and flax, were accordingly put together in haste by the river side; and the funeral procession was on the point of commencing, when the Resident sent a servant of his own to make a final effort to dissuade the victim. The messenger found the Brahmins plying her with camphor, and was wholly unable to overcome the natural and artificial exaltation which she exhibited. Moreover, the crowd were impatient at what they deemed so pertinacious an opposition to the Divine will, and bore the woman off to the palace, in order to obtain the chief's prohibition of any further attempts of the kind. The messenger had the courage to accompany them. On being admitted to the presence, he reminded his Highness of his late promise to the Resident; but his remonstrances were quickly neutralised by an adroit hint to the prince from a native courtier, that "if the widow's purpose were thwarted, she might utter some imprecations fatal to the State!" On this, his Highness declared that he would stand neutral in the matter—"he would neither assent nor dissent—the messenger might do his best." The Brahmins and crowd, of course, interpreted this as it was meant; they jostled the emissaries of the chargé d'affaires, and even threw out threats against that officer himself, in case of any further interference. Musicians now came out from the palace to assist at the ceremony; a sumptuous dress and ornaments were presented to the woman; and, thus decorated and attended, she was conducted to the place of sacrifice. Secret orders to use despatch had, in the meantime, been sent by the Prince; and so well were these obeyed, that within three hours of Luchmun Brahmin's death, his widow had shared his obsequies.

It is true that cases have occurred more horrible than those above related. Instances are on record, in which, at the supreme moment, women have lost courage, and, starting from the pile, have torn off their sacrificial garlands, and cried aloud for mercy! Unhappily, too, it is not improbable that, on some of these occasions, the fatal belief that a Suttee's resolution once voluntarily taken is irrevocable, may have caused the bystanders to thrust the victim remorselessly back into the flames; or if, from British interposition, a rescue has been effected, the woman has, it may be, survived only to curse the pity which, to save her from a few moments of pain, has deprived her, as she deemed, of ages of happiness.* These things have been; but, with rare exceptions, the Suttee is a voluntary victim. Resolute, undismayed, confident in her own inspiration, but betraying by the tone of her prophecies—which are almost always auspicious—and by the gracious acts with which she takes leave of her household, and by the gifts which she lavishes on the bystanders, that her tender woman's heart is the true source whence that inspiration flows, the child-widow has scarcely time to bewail her husband ere she makes ready to rejoin him. She is dressed like a bride, but it is as a bride who has been re-

* In some cases Suttee is performed without the aid of fire, by burying the widow alive. For the particulars of this form of the rite, see Ward's *View of the History, &c., of the Hindoos*, vol. i. p. lxxi. and vol. ii. p. 110.

ceived within the zenána of her bridegroom. Her veil is put off, her hair unbound; and so adorned, and so exposed, she goes forth to gaze on the world for the first time, face to face, ere she leaves it. She does not blush or quail. She scarcely regards the bearded crowd who press so eagerly towards *her*. Her lips move in momentary prayer. Paradise is in her view. She sees her husband awaiting with approbation the sacrifice which shall restore her to him dowered with the expiation of their sins, and ennobled with a martyr's crown. What wonder if, dazzled with these visionary glories, she heeds not the shouting throng, the ominous pile? Exultingly she mounts the last earthly couch which she shall share with her lord. His head she places fondly on her lap. The priests set up their chant—it is a strange hymeneal—and her first-born son, walking thrice round the pile, lights the flame. If the impulse which can suffice to steel a woman's nerves to encounter so painful a death, and to overpower the yearnings of her heart towards the children she may leave behind her—if such an impulse is, even to the eye of philosophy, a strange evidence of the power of faith, and of the depth and strength of tenderness—surely we may well conceive how the superstitious Hindoo should trace in it more directly the finger of God Himself. They, we are persuaded, will best cope with this superstition—for they alone will comprehend the grounds on which it rests—who, content with the weapons of truth, will own, that love, and beauty, and death—terror, wonder, pity—never conspired to form a rite more solemn and affecting to the untutored heart of man.*

The confirmation that the Kotah case appeared to give to the current opinions on the danger of interference, had naturally caused

* "I have heard," says Mr. Mountstuart Elphinstone, "that in Guzerat women about to burn are often stupified with opium. In most other parts this is certainly not the case. Women go through all the ceremonies with astonishing composure and presence of mind, and have been seen seated, unconfined, among the flames, apparently praying, and raising their joined hands to their heads with as little agitation as at their ordinary devotions. The sight of a widow burning is a most painful one; but it is hard to say whether the spectator is most affected by pity or admiration. The more than human serenity of the victim, and the respect which she receives from all around her, are heightened by her gentle demeanor and her care to omit nothing in distributing her last presents, and paying the usual marks of courtesy to the bystanders; while the cruel death that awaits her is doubly felt from her own apparent insensibility to its terrors."—*History of India*, i. 361.

an official neutrality on the subject to be prescribed more strictly than ever to our Residents at the native courts; and a complete inaction was the order of the day. Not to multiply instances of this policy, we may mention that, in 1842, Lord Ellenborough expressly declined to sanction an offer made by the chargé d'affaires at Hyderabad, to procure from its Mahomedan ruler a prohibition of the rite.

It was in the midst of this general despondency that Major (now Lieutenant-Colonel) Ludlow, chargé d'affaires at Jypore, conceived the idea of assailing the superstition in its stronghold. His scheme was simple, and not new—qualities which are the best evidence of the difficulties that had hitherto prevented its execution. Long ago, Oriental scholars, both native and European, had shown that the rite was not only unsanctioned, but inferentially forbidden, by the earliest and most authoritative Hindoo scriptures.* Nay, Colonel Tod, in his book on Rajpootána, had actually

* A corrupt passage in the Rig-Veda is the only primitive authority that has ever been adduced in favour of Suttee, and receives, indeed, this interpretation from Mr. Colebrooke in the fourth volume of the *Asiatic Researches*, p. 211. See, however, POSTSCRIPT, p. 58.

indicated this anomaly in Hindoo doctrine as the best point of attack for abolitionists to select. Yet, though that valuable work was published in 1829, and though the author, from the position he long held as chief diplomatic officer in the country he so well describes, had the amplest opportunities for carrying out his own suggestion, it was reserved for Major Ludlow, in 1844, to put it to the test of practice, and to vanquish the obstacles which had hitherto confined it to the dream-land of speculative benevolence.

The explanation of this previous inaction is not difficult. Scholars, it is true, had proved Suttee to be an innovation and a heresy; but it was an innovation of 2000 years' standing, and a heresy abetted by the priesthood since the days of Alexander. Though unnoticed by Menu, the supplementary writings with which the Hindoos, like the Jews, have overlaid their primitive books, are profuse in its praise. Above all—let the force of the appeal from the more recent to the primitive code be what it might—it could not but be attended with suspicion when proceeding from religionists who equally repudiated both the one and the other. It is no matter for surprise, that Englishmen should have hesitated long to assail with the delicate weapon of theological criticism a rite thus strong in remote antiquity, in venerated records, in a hierarchy at once ignorant and unscrupulous, and in the associations with which innumerable traditions of womanly courage and constancy had ennobled it in the eyes of the Hindoo people.

His resolution once taken, however, there were circumstances in Major Ludlow's position not unfavourable to the enterprise. He enjoyed peculiar opportunities of intercourse with the nobles of the court to which he was accredited. The prince of Jypore was a minor, and the government was carried on by a council of regency, over which the Major presided. Not only did he thus possess a more direct voice in the administration than his post of chargé d'affaires would have given him, but he had already so used this vantage-ground as to dissipate, to an extraordinary degree, the jealousies likely to be excited in his native colleagues by any interference with their domestic customs. He had even contrived to bring the other Rajpoot states to combine with

Jypore for an object not wholly alien from that which he had at present in view. Then, as now, the abuse which he had undertaken to assail concerned their zenánas; and his bitterest opponents were likely to be found amongst the priests.

Old maids, as our readers have probably heard, are sadly depreciated in the East. A Rajpoot girl who remains long unwedded is a disgrace to her house; but that was not the only danger which, but a few years ago, her father had to fear. Should he succeed in finding her a husband, the chances were, that the family estates would be hopelessly encumbered in providing the gratuities claimed by the priests and minstrels who were certain to flock to the nuptials. No Rajpoot is above the dread of satire and imprecations; and those worthies notoriously dispensed their blessings and applauses, or their curses and lampoons, according to the price at which their services were retained. The result was, that their favour was purchased at almost any cost. "The Dáhima emptied his coffers on the marriage of his daughter"—ran a favourite distich of these venal bards—"but he filled them with the praises of mankind!" The Rajpoots at large were not disposed to be Dáhimas, nor yet to brave the scandal of housing marriageable daughters. They found refuge from the dilemma in infanticide. Parents reared just so many girls as they could afford to marry off, and destroyed the rest. The criminality of the practice was, indeed, acknowledged. Rajpoot decorum demanded that it should be veiled in secrecy; but that was all. A trifling penance absolved the perpetrator. Nobody dreamed of dragging such affairs into publicity. If a son was born, the fact was announced to inquirers with exultation; if a daughter, the answer was—*Nothing!* and those who came to congratulate went silent away. At the same time, it must not be supposed that this system had grown up to such monstrous maturity without some degree of resistance on the part of the native rulers. It appears that here and there, and at various periods, a Rajpoot prince had sought to reach the evil by sumptuary enactments in restraint of nuptial gratuities; but that fear of the reproach of their kinsmen in neighbouring communities had invariably deterred his subjects from taking advantage of the remedy.

Major Ludlow conceived that he saw his

way to improving on these precedents. He conjectured that, if the various states throughout Rajpootána could be brought to agree to a *common* scale of such largesses, apportioned to the revenue of the bride's parents, and with uniform penalties for all demands in excess, the problem might be solved. Nothing, however, is harder than to bring these tenacious principalities to act together on any subject. What could seem more so than to bring them to work in concert on a question involving points so delicate as the largesses to be dispensed on their daughters' weddings, and the comparative claims of their minstrels and priests? It was certain, too, that, failing this agreement, no measure of the kind could be demanded of them by the British Government without a breach of the treaties that secured the freedom of their internal administrations.

In spite of these obstacles, Major Ludlow obtained permission to do his best, on the single condition of using no direct solicitation towards the chiefs. His first efforts were thus confined to his brother diplomatists, and to such native deputies as resided at Jypore for the purpose of communuicating on plunder-cases. The latter, gradually coming into the idea, promulgated it among their respective governments; and, by this indirect process, he at length succeeded in obtaining the enactment of an international sumptuary law which has rid Rajpootána of its most frightful scourge and stigma.

Never probably before, since the origin of the Rajpoot States, had their jealousies and divisions been even temporarily suspended. But the advantage of their tardy concert was at once rendered palpable to them by their delivery from a ruinous system of extortion, with all its frightful and unnatural results. They were aware that the merit of this social, rather than political, reform, was due to Major Ludlow's private exertions; and thus between him and themselves there sprung up a relation on such subjects, which the antipathies of race and religion very seldom allow of amongst Englishmen and Hindoos. What, then, if he could avail himself of these aids to accomplish an infinitely harder undertaking? He had rid the Rajpoots of a practice which their consciences condemned. Could he rid them of one to the full as terrible, which they revered? He had rescued her child for the mother. Could he rescue the mother for the child? It was, doubtless, much for an Englishman to hope to tear aside the prescriptive sanctions which, for twenty centuries, had elevated the Indian widow's cruel martyrdom into the holiest of mysteries; but if the shock was ever to be given, it was now, and at Jypore. The resident Vakeels would communicate it to all the Rajpoot States; and whenever Rajpootána should lead the way in breaking through "the traditions of the elders," Hindostan at large was tolerably certain to follow.

The hour, the place, and the man, all favoured the design. One lion, however, there was in the path. Major Ludlow could not hope that the permission given him to use his personal influence with the convention of Vakeels to promote measures against female infanticide, would be extended to any similar undertaking against Suttee. The acknowledged criminality of the one practice, and the reputed sanctity of the other, made here all the difference; and we have already alluded to the belief on the part of the British authorities, which so many facts had seemed to substantiate, that the efforts of our diplomatists in the independent states to check the rite had tended only to an opposite effect. As an essential condition therefore to success, and on pain of having his operations summarily suspended, Major Ludlow was compelled to work unseen.

He determined, if possible, to induce two or three trustworthy and influential natives to undertake the cause; to ply *them* with the critical objection drawn from the older Scriptures; and, by declaring his own resolution to remain neutral till public opinion had declared itself, to excite in them the ambition of taking the lead. He found a person admirably adapted to his purpose in the Financial Minister of the court at which he was accredited. Seth Manick Chund belonged to a sect whose distaste for destruction in all its forms is singular even in the East. The Oswal tribe do not wilfully slay the meanest animal. Carrying out the doctrine of the transmigration of souls to its logical result—viewing in every insect a possible human intelligence, and as yet blissfully ignorant of the revelations of the oxy-hydrogen microscope—their priests carry besoms to sweep the ground on which they tread, and cover their mouths with gauze, to avoid the scandal of inhaling their ancestors, or of crushing them wholesale under foot! One result of this tenderness for life in every shape is, that they disapprove of Suttees. To the Financial Minister, therefore, and to his own head Moonshee, Major Ludlow communicated all the arguments he thought likely to be of use; and, thus charged, they betook themselves to the High Priest of Jypore.

Warily, and as if on their own account, they pressed this important dignitary with the omission of all mention of Suttee in the Code of Menu; with the inferential prohibition of the rite in the denunciations contained in that work against suicide; and with its promise to widows *living* chastely of eternal felicity with their husbands—whereas even the writings which countenanced the sacrifice, limited the duration of its recompense to the comparative *bagatelle* of thirty-five millions of years! * In

* "There are 35,000,000 hairs on the human body. The woman who ascends the pile with her husband will remain so many years in heaven."—Hindoo quotation, in Ward's *View of the History, &c., of the Hindoos*, vol. ii. p. 96.

addition to these objections, already familiar to Oriental scholars, Major Ludlow supplied his emissaries with two others at least as efficacious. Pope's Universal Prayer embodies, it appears, a favourite sentiment of Hindoo moralists:—

> "What conscience dictates to be done,
> Or warns me not to do;
> This teach me more than hell to shun,
> That *more than Heaven* pursue."

But the Hindoo divines assert, not only that the love of goodness for its own sake ought to *prevail* over the hopes of posthumous reward, but that the slightest intrusion of an interested motive is fatal. What more easy than to apply this dogma to the poor widow bent on earning by a cruel death her own, and her husband's, salvation? Her devotion was represented as a mercenary calculation of profit and loss. She did but mock the Deity with the unclean sacrifice of a selfish bargain. Was the martyr's crown her aim? She had forfeited it by that very aspiration!

Major Ludlow wound up these arguments by a shrewd appeal to national pride. 'Suttee (urged his emissaries), unwarranted by Menu, was the evident invention of some degenerate race whose women were worthless, and whose widows, if they survived, would bring reproach on the memory of their lords. To such it might be left. The honour of Rajpoot husbands was in safer keeping; and the fair fame of their daughters was aspersed by the mere retention of so disgraceful a security!

The High Priest received these representations with surprising candour. In less than six months, he was induced to put forth a document, in which he adopted all the theological arguments, and declared authoritatively, that the self-immolation of widows was less meritorious than their practising "the living Suttee of chastity and devotion!" This was evidently half the battle. Major Ludlow now personally entered into the contest, so far as to cause the manifesto to be shown at his residence to the various Vakeels who came there to transact business; and these, in their turn, communicated its contents to their masters. A religious agitation sprung up, and spread widely. At the same time, there could be little doubt that, let the impression produced by the High Priest's decision be what it might, no man of rank—least of all, a Rajpoot Sovereign—would be anxious to proclaim himself the first convert.

To iterate day by day the same arguments—to be ever on the stretch to discover methods of rendering them more efficient—to confirm the wavering—to encourage those who were already compromised as abolitionists—above all, to keep within the delicate line that severed his private advocacy of the High Priest's dictum from his official adhesion to it—here was an arduous combination of aims; and the Major knew that if he failed in any one of them, a quick and mischievous reaction of public opinion would render the object of all his toil more distant than ever, and expose him to the censure of his own Government. But what then? It was the old alternative of every man wiser and braver than his fellows—the criterion would be success. If he did not win the palm of a benefactor of his race, he must be content to be reproached as a meddler whose untimely zeal had but injured a noble cause.

Within a few months of the issue of the High Priest's manifesto, that personage died.

Never, not even during his last sickness, did he receive the slightest message or civility from Major Ludlow. So important was it deemed to give no ground for the imputation of a secret understanding between them. While, therefore, it was part of the good fortune attending this enterprise, that the High Priest should have left the scene in the odour of sanctity before he had leisure to retract or modify his opinion, it was probably due to Major Ludlow's caution, that the public faith in the honesty of the manifesto remained to the last unshaken.

And now the fruit of all this untiring energy began to appear. One by one, the members of the Council of Regency declared themselves in favour of the legal prohibition of Suttee; though they did not as yet think proper to pledge the infant sovereign to so critical a measure. Most of the nobles connected with the Court were avowed abolitionists, and three of the tributary provinces of Jypore actually issued enactments against the rite. Their example was followed by several petty neighbouring states.

Major Ludlow believed that the time was

come for bolder measures. Every thing depended on the utmost publicity being given to the adhesions he had already received. Great as was the general respect for the deceased High Priest's authority, the timid were not likely to be converted except in good company, and, as has been said, the timidest of all in a matter of Rajpoot orthodoxy would be the Rajpoot sovereigns. He was aware, indeed, that rumour had already befriended him in this respect. The resident Vakeels had, as a matter of course, kept their masters throughout Rajpootána well acquainted with the progress of the strange agitation at Jypore. But those functionaries had no access to the letters which, in his capacity of President of the Council of Regency, he had from time to time received from the leading abolitionists; and such documents, forming collectively a very imposing record of opinion in high places, had now accumulated in his hands. These he resolved to turn to account. He sent copies of the whole correspondence to two or three of his brother diplomatists in Rajpootána, in order that they might communicate it to the Courts to which they were attached. The result was—his first and only check. His official superior, apprised of the circulation of these documents, took alarm, and arrested the whole proceeding. The mortification to Ludlow must have been great; but there remained so much to be done, and by means so foreign to the routine of official experience, that we can scarcely be astonished that the first impression inspired by the promulgation of the plan should have been one of distrust. When, however, a year had passed without any evil resulting from the agitation of the subject, the able officer who had thus felt it his duty to interpose his authority, so far withdrew his opposition as to issue a circular to the chiefs, urging, on the grounds already taken, not indeed the prohibition of Suttee, but the imposition of penalties on all persons abetting the widow in the rite.

Happily, the event surpassed these cautious advances, and proved how little Major Ludlow had overrated the strength of the movement. In eight months' time from the issuing of the circular (August 23rd, 1846), *the Council of Regency at Jypore led the way among the great independent Rajpoot states in declaring Suttee* *penal on all parties engaged in it, principals as well as accessories.* Lord Hardinge, then at Simla, at once caused a notification of this event, coupled with an expression of thanks to Major Ludlow, to be published in the Government Gazette (Sept. 22, 1846); and so vast, and so swift, was the effect of this example, and of the prominence thus judiciously assigned to it, that, before Christmas, his Lordship was enabled to announce the prohibition of Suttee by eleven, out of the eighteen, Rajpoot principalities, and by five, out of the remaining sixteen, free states of India! Of the whole territory then exempt from internal control, more than two-thirds were gained over to the cause of abolition within four months from the Jypore proclamation.*

* The following table gives, we believe, with a tolerable approach to accuracy, a view of the progress up to the present time (May, 1855), of the cause of abolition among those states which have the control of their internal affairs :—

Abolitionist (19).

| *Rajpootána.* | Square Miles. |
|---|---|
| Jypore | 13,427 |
| Kotah | 3,102 |
| Jhálawar | 1,287 |
| Boondee | 2,291 |
| Jessulmere | 9,779 |
| Banswarra | 1,440 |

To persons unacquainted with the influence of Rajpootána on Hindostan, so sudden an inter-

| *Rajpootána.* | Square Miles. |
|---|---|
| Brought forward - - - | 31,326 |
| Purtabgurh - - - | 1,457 |
| Doongurpore - - - | 2,005 |
| Kerowlee - - - - | 1,870 |
| Sirohee - - - - | 3,024 |
| Dholepore - - - | 1,626 |
| Ameer Khan (Mahomedan) - - | 1,633 |
| Jodhpore - - - - | 34,132 |
| Total - - - | 77,073 |
| *Out of Rajpootána.* | |
| Hyderabad (Mahomedan) - - | 88,887 |
| Indore (Mahratta) - - - | 4,245 |
| Rewah (Rajpoot) - - - | 10,310 |
| Bundelkund - - - | 16,173 |
| Gwalior (Mahratta) - - - | 32,944 |
| Cashmere - - about | 1,500 |
| Total area - - - | 231,132 |

NON-ABOLITIONIST (15).

| *Rajpootána.* | Square Miles. |
|---|---|
| Meywar - - - - | 11,784 |
| Ulwur - - - - | 3,235 |
| Bikaneer - - - - | 18,060 |
| Kishengurh - - - | 724 |
| Bhurtpore (Jaut) - - - | 1,946 |
| Total - - | 35,749 |
| *Out of Rajpootána.* | |
| Baroda (Mahratta) - - - | 5,525 |
| Katteewar (Rajpoot) - | 19,424 |

ruption of the torpor of ages might well have appeared too momentous to be ascribed to the seemingly simple measures at Jypore which it immediately followed. It was as if Major Ludlow had thrown a pebble from the shore, and the ice of an arctic sea had riven before him. Yet never did a train of events less deserve to be ranked as mere coincidences. If any further proof were necessary, we might point to the fact that the state of Gwalior, in

| *Out of Rajpootána.* | Square Miles. |
|---|---|
| Brought forward - - - | 60,698 |
| Bhopal (Mahomedan) - - | 6,772 |
| Cutch (Rajpoot) - - - | 7,396 |
| Dhar (Rajpoot) - - - | 1,465 |
| Sawuntwarree (Mahratta) - - | 935 |
| The four protected Sikh States - | 16,602 |
| Total area - - - | 93,868 |

Kotah did not give in its adhesion until March, 1847; Jodhpore followed during Lord Dalhousie's administration; while Indore is stated to have prohibited the rite so long ago as the reign of Hurree Rao Holkar. The last mentioned prohibition had, indeed, remained unheard of elsewhere down to the date of the proclamation at Jypore; but this may be explained by the slight importance likely to be attached by Hindoos in general to the religious proceedings of a community of Mahrattas. The Sikh empire, which, with the exception of Cashmere, has since been annexed to the British dominions, is included among the five abolitionist States out of Rajpootána, alluded to in our text.

proclaiming Suttee penal, expressly cited as its authority the edict from Jypore; while nearly every abolitionist sovereign assigned as the grounds of his adhesion, the very arguments that had obtained the Jypore high-priest's sanction. The recognition of Major Ludlow's services by his own superior was immediate and hearty: — "The last Political Agent" — wrote Colonel Sutherland to the Government— "was, I believe, as little prepared for the abolition of Suttee at Jypore as I was on my return to that capital in May, 1846; and it is almost exclusively to Major Ludlow's influence that we are indebted for the first promulgation of the law prohibiting Suttee in a Hindoo principality."* Major Ludlow's aids were, a superior utterly incapable of petty jealousies, and ready to abandon his own anti-abolitionist views directly abolition appeared possible; a variety of British officers residing at other native courts, eager to forward the good work when once begun; a Governor-General capable of appreciating the lustre which such an achievement would cast on an administration

* From the Governor-General's Agent for Rajpootána to the Secretary to Government, September 11, 1847.

already bright with military glories; and last, not least, a Court of Directors ever prompt in the recognition of great services.

Our narrative is concluded. It would be a strangely superficial view that saw in it nothing but a skilful series of measures by which a certain annual saving of female life has been effected, to the gain of Eastern morality, and to the credit of the chief actor. The great fact it teaches is, that *the Hindoo mind is capable of advance even in the department where its immobility has been deemed most absolute — traditionary faith.*

More than threescore years have passed since Burke thus described our Indian Empire: —

"With us, are no retributory superstitions by which a foundation of charity compensates through ages to the poor for the rapine and injustice of a day. With us no pride erects stately monuments, which repair the mischiefs that pride had produced, and which adorn a country out of its own spoils. England has erected no churches, no hospitals, no palaces, no schools. England has built no bridges, made no high-roads, cut no navigations, dug out no reservoirs. Every other conqueror of every other description has left some monument either of state or beneficence behind him. Were *we* to be driven out of India this day, nothing would remain to tell that it had been possessed, during the inglorious period of our dominion, by anything better than the ourang-outang or the tiger."

Doubtless, when this eloquent invective was uttered, many of the "monuments" desiderated by the orator were due at our hands; and great and valuable have been the efforts since made in recognition of the debt. But Burke himself did not dream of *moral* memorials, of records traced in the faith and customs of the people. It may be questioned, indeed, whether he did not hold them superfluous. "This multitude of men" — he said of the natives of India on the same occasion — "does not consist of an abject and barbarous populace, but a people for ages civilized and cultivated — cultivated by all the arts of polished life whilst we were in the woods." There, in truth, has lain the difficulty of their making any further advance. It was this very polish — a polish of luxury rather than of civilization — a polish of surface incompatible with growth — that, like the glittering cement encasing the Pyramids, preserved the primeval institutions of Hindostan through twenty centuries of rapine and subjection, proof alike to the whirling wastes of barbarism and the keen assaults of Western intellect. It was the inveterate complacency, sprung from this very idea that they possessed most of the arts of peace when the rest of mankind were "in the woods," which had convinced them that nothing remained to add to their mental stores, and that to arrange and adorn their existing materials was for ever their only duty. Nay, so absolute was this state of optimism, that no one custom or tenet was held less indisputably excellent than another; since all derived their importance from the common sanction of antiquity. A change in a Hindoo's food or his faith, in his *poojah* or his porridge, was equally odious to him — equally a reflection on the infallibility of his forefathers — to question which, were indeed "confusion worse than death."

That the semibarbarous conquerors from northern Asia, whose "retributory superstitions" Burke has eulogised, should have been able to break into so compact a system, was not, perhaps, to be expected. India rather influenced them than they India, and, like a voluptuous mistress, enervated each in turn, till he resigned her to some hardier captor. But even the European invaders, who were saved from such a fate, if by no other cause, by this — that their physical constitution precluded them from settling on the soil — even they, with all the energy which a constant recruiting of the governing class from the West secured to their respective dynasties, had never, until the period of our narrative, broken one of the links in the ancient chain of Hindoo *dustoor.* The distressing failures of our own missionaries are notorious. " How" — wrote the zealous but truthful Henry Martin, after more than a year's fruitless labour on that impracticable soil —

"How shall it ever be possible to convince a Hindoo or Brahmin of anything? . . . . Truly, if ever I see a Hindoo a real believer in Jesus, I shall see something more nearly approaching the resurrection of a dead body than anything I have yet seen. This last week a Brahmin came three or four days following, and stayed an hour or two each time. I told him all that God had done for mankind from the beginning; the evidence of Christianity, the nature of it, the folly and wickedness of their religion; in short, every topic that could affect a human being. At the end of all he was exactly as at the beginning: *the same serene smile denotes the absence of all feeling.*"—*Journal*, p. 536.

And again, a year and a half later :—" Were

the Hindoo woman you mention a true convert, she would be a rich reward for a life's labour; but alas! I doubt of every Hindostanee Christian in Hindostan" (*Ib.*, p. 628). This opinion seems to have been shared by Sir James Mackintosh:—"He thought that little was to be apprehended and little hoped for from the exertions of the missionaries" (*Ib.*, p. 706).

It is true that, by dint of unflagging efforts, the pioneers of the Gospel in the East have attained—in Southern India especially—a degree of success which would have astonished Martin. But the sum of conversions, when viewed with reference to the number of our subjects, is as a drop in the ocean. And how, in effect, can a people who conceive themselves to be living in a very atmosphere of miracles, celestial and diabolical, attach adequate importance to the evidence of those wonders by which the divine origin of Christianity is attested? On the other hand, if they are to judge us by "our fruits," what are the qualities likely to attract their regard? In our preachers they see none of that terrible asceticism with which the naked fakeer, or self-torturing jogee, successfully challenges their reverence. The exposure of our women's faces, the indiscriminate mixture of the sexes in our social meetings, our dancing, our unscrupulous diet, are, each of them, features which, however innocent in themselves, shock that material morality which the natives best appreciate. They admit, indeed, our veracity, justice, and energy, and that "beaver-like" faculty which one of our own satirists has seized as the principal national attribute. That it is our destiny, for some inscrutable purpose, to make our penknives bristle from pole to pole, to run a girdle round the earth with our printed yarns, and to fight, if need be, for these objects like Roostums, or scheme like Faridoons—all these things are admitted by the natives, and the contemplation of them fills them with wonder and awe. But alas! no less true is it, that none of these things move their envy. If, therefore, success in teaching the Hindoo a higher and truer civilization is possible at all, our first efforts must be directed towards convincing them of the defects of their own system, rather than of the merits of ours—when they can appreciate the last, the battle will have been won.

Eight years ago, to a proposal even thus limited, nobody could have been blamed for objecting with Henry Martin, "How shall it ever be possible to convince a Hindoo of anything?" But who can say that it is hopeless *now*, when half the states of Hindostan have been brought to repudiate a rite which was held holy by their race for full three centuries before the Christian era? True, the arguments which have effected the change, have been of a kind that left the validity of their ancient books unassailed—nay, the doctrine of one series has been abandoned mainly, if not solely, on account of its incompatibility with still older and more venerated authorities. But it is surely needless to point out the consequences of admitting reason, in whatsoever guise, into the domain of tradition. Call it mere comparative criticism, if we will—the truth remains equally obvious, that criticism, once sanctioned in any form, will in the end detect something more than the discrepancies between rival records. Let us, then, appreciate our vantage-ground. The small end of the wedge is inserted—how are we to drive it home?

In the first place, we would suggest the importance of making the significance of the movement in its bearings on the fallibility both of tradition and of the priesthood, as apparent to the whole Hindoo family as it is to ourselves. Let the present generation be made to understand, however much the effort may cost them, that they have veritably declared and proved themselves wiser than all their predecessors since the date of the Shasters. Let them perceive, that it is not only harmless, but good, to exercise reason—at any rate for the purpose of reviving the primeval wisdom of the Code. And we may fairly hope that Hindoo intellect, having once exercised its wings so far, will not fold them up for ever afterwards in serene contemplation of the age of Menu.*

In the next place, let us guard against relapse. Before now there have been native rulers, more enlightened, or less devout, than their subjects, who have endeavoured to put

* Facilities will, ere very long, be afforded to the natives for remounting to yet more ancient authorities than Menu.—See POSTSCRIPT.

down the most cruel among the Hindoo rites. But, whatever effect their enactments may have had during their own reigns, the flood of popular superstition invariably rolled back afterwards, and their laws soon sank into matters of history. To avoid this danger, our Government should be constantly on the watch to see that its abolitionist allies carry out their own proclamations. Marks of favour might reward every display of zeal in this direction; while reactionaries might be made to understand, that we regarded their adhesion to the cause of humanity as in some sort a compact with ourselves.

Finally, there is now before us in Rajpootána an excellent opening for educating the higher classes of natives of the independent states of Northern India. The schools at Agra, and at Calcutta, are too remote for their benefits to reach these influential principalities. We possess in Ajmere, situated as it is in the midst of Rajpootána, a small tract of territory admirably adapted for the purpose. Not only is it advisable, in choosing a site for such a foundation, to prefer the vicinity of a race who, more widely than any other, influence the mind of Hindostan — but it also happens, that the Rajpoots are, of all our allies, the most likely to accept the benefits of education at our hands. This is due, in part, to the confidence which our respect for their liberties, ever since we first rescued their country from the Mahratta yoke, has inspired; in part, to the increased facilities for making pilgrimages to distant shrines afforded by our roads; which, by familiarising them with the superior fertility and order of the British territory, have already stimulated in them a degree of curiosity as to the secret of our advantages. Great numbers of Rajpoots have accepted vaccination from us, at the risk of offending one of the direst divinities in their Pantheon — Mátajee, the *goddess of small-pox!* Above all, they have now been the first to cooperate with us in putting down Suttee. Such are the tokens, both of greater independence of spirit, and of amity towards ourselves, which have satisfied those most competent to judge, that the higher Rajpoots would gladly lead the way in making use of a college at Ajmere. The only educational experiment hitherto made there, was at a period when our relations, both at Jypore and Jodhpore, were on the most unfriendly footing. Of course, it failed. But under no circumstances would it have availed for the objects now indicated. What is wanted in the first instance, is not so much a school for the lower orders, as a college to which the chiefs can send their sons, accompanied by something of that state and retinue which native nobles consider essential to their rank. The lecturers should be gentlemen—men of habitual courtesy. Honorary privileges connected with the foundation might be placed within reach of the leading Rajpoots, who would, in all probability, forward the scheme in proportion as it appeared to identify them with the Supreme Government. No religious instruction should, at first, be attempted. This proviso is essential. You may write Christianity, or any other faith, on the *tabula rasa* of a savage mind—with a people, not in the infancy of barbarism, but in the decrepitude of a precocious civilisation, you have to unteach before you can teach; and an interval must occur between the two processes. The direct extrusion of one religion by another absolutely distinct, after the fashion of the pellets of a popgun, is too rare and exceptional to be anticipated anywhere, least of all in India. Nor can the miraculous extension of Christianity, in primitive times, be so good a guide to us here as the local experience of our own propagandists. There is, we fear, almost of necessity, a sceptical period that supervenes on the tearing up of the old belief which has wound its roots round all a man's thoughts and associations; and he is happy in whose life the truth can spring from the soil so disturbed by the eradication of falsehood. It is, perhaps, possible that our efforts to educate the Hindoos may not do more than destroy idolatry in one generation; and that the intolerable want of *something to hold by* will not necessitate the adoption of Christianity in its place till the next. Be that as it may, we must remember that the choice is not between religious and secular education for the Hindoos, but between secular education and none at all. We must do what we can to give that enlightenment which will be adequate to discover the deformities of error, and *then*, perchance, our pupils may learn to see the beauties of truth.

We do not envy the man who can see nothing in the career thus opening before England in the East but hazard to her empire. "Once teach the natives"—some reasoners have urged—"the absurdities of their divisions of caste and creed, and we shall lose the chief security for our power." It is enough to answer, that England holds her possessions of God, not of the devil; and that the world has never seen a satanic counsel answer in the long run. The future may be dark, but it will not be dangerous, so long as our conduct is guided by the principle that Morals and Policy cannot be antagonistic. What, in fine, has been our experience in India? One by one, the worst reproaches in its administration have disappeared; extortion, corruption, and cruelty are matters of the past; and, in the same degree, the loyalty of our native subjects, the deference of our allies, and the confusion of our enemies have become more and more conspicuous. It is thus, and not by the selfish calculations that marked its origin, that our Eastern empire has grown to be a wonder of the world. Like a coralline island, its foundations were laid by petty agencies, working for ends they knew not of. But the storm and the sunshine, and the dews of heaven, have descended on the harsh superstructure, and softened and ripened it into a generous soil — needing, of a truth, abundant husbandry—but already rich with increase, and full of promise.

# POSTSCRIPT.

---

The foregoing narrative is founded on unpublished official documents, to the study of which the writer brought the advantage of having served in Rajpootána for nearly three years, in a subordinate diplomatic post. Compelled by ill health to retire early from India, he was glad thus to discharge, however inadequately, a portion of the debt due to his late profession.

The time seems to have come for again bringing the subjects above treated before the public. Since September, 1851, Oriental scholars have dealt more than one heavy blow to eastern superstition. In the first place, a step has been taken towards enabling the Hindoo to judge for himself of the glaring discrepancies between his present faith and the primitive records on which it assumes to be based. Usually ignorant of the very language of his ancient hymns, or Vedas — the recitation of which is, nevertheless, strictly enjoined — the Brahmin is further debarred from ascertaining their meaning by their broken and elliptical text. Still he obeys the injunction; and sometimes he recites them forwards, and sometimes — with a variety of resource that recalls the mediæval device for raising the devil — he recites them backwards. What will be the bewilderment of the devotee when he shall learn, from their perusal in his native tongue, that they are addressed to beings who figure no longer as the *di majores* of his Pantheon; that the greatest gods and goddesses of modern Hindostan have no place whatever in these venerated Vedas; that castes are unrecognized by them, metempsychosis ignored, and the incarnation of Vishnu, and the tri-une mystery itself, not once adumbrated!* Such a discovery can

* For a learned account of these records, which are supposed to be coeval with the Pentateuch itself—and of the evidence afforded by them of the Scythian origin of the Hindoo race — see Professor Wilson's Prefaces to his Translations of the First and Second Books of the *Rig-Veda* (Wm. H. Allen and Co.).

scarcely fail of proving fatal to the existing superstition, and will certainly not revive that which is dead; for whatever else may come of the shock, it may safely be predicted, the Hindoo wil not revert to the Vedaic eleme ts —he will not learn his faith backwards, like his hymns.

This mighty disenchantment may be said to be even now in preparation. By the wise liberality of the East India Company, Dr. Max Müller and Professor Wilson have been enabled to devote themselves, the one to collating the text of the Rig-Veda, and the other to rendering it into English; whence, of course, it can easily be translated into the modern dialects of Hindostan. The second instalment of this great work has recently been given to the world; and deeply is it to be hoped, that a task which has never before been more than partially performed, and which few are competent to undertake at all, is destined to be completed by the accomplished scholars who have now entered upon it.

Perhaps it falls more strictly within the scope of this narrative to notice, that a discovery has been made, during the course of their joint labours, which supplies the last link to the argument for considering widow-burning a spurious Hindoo rite. It has been ascertained that an obscure passage in the Rig-Veda, occasionally adduced as the one primitive authority for Suttee, is so far from really having any such character, that it enjoins inferentially the widow's preservation. The absence of any allusion to the rite in a work so full of reference to the Vedas as the Code of Menu, together with the rules of holy living laid down for widows by that law-giver, had, indeed, already thrown the utmost doubt upon the text in question.* But it was reserved for Professor Wilson to change doubt into certainty, and so to demolish the last Brahminical pretext for regarding Suttee as an orthodox Hindoo practice. In a paper read by the learned Professor before the Royal Asiatic Society, on February the 4th, 1854, he pointed out that the disputed passage had, in fact, been corrupted by the substitution of the word *agneh* for *agreh* — the meaning being thereby perverted from "let

* See page 21.

them [the widows] go up into the *dwelling*," to "let them go up into the *fire*"—a flagrant corruption truly. Professor Wilson added, that he was supported in this opinion by Dr. Max Müller; and that Aswalayana, the author of the "Grihya Sutras"—a work little inferior in authority to the Vedas themselves—actually designates the proper person for leading the widow away at the conclusion of the funeral-rites.

There is evidently no time to be lost in acquainting those native rulers who, during Lord Hardinge's administration, refused to abolish Suttee, with this new ground on which they may reconsider the question without compromising the reasoning then put forward by them to justify their recusancy. The Court of Directors are understood to have sent out numerous copies of Professor Wilson's paper for distribution among their diplomatic servants; but it remains to be seen what efforts the Indian Government will make to turn to account the new instrument for good thus unexpectedly supplied.

Unhappily, the fact cannot be concealed that the cause of Suttee-abolition has, of late years, received in India no fresh impulse, if, indeed, it has not actually retrograded. With the single exception of Jodhpore, no new adhesions on the part of the native states have to be added to those enumerated in the preceding pages. Yet all the gravest difficulties have been surmounted; and vigilance and energy in the path already opened, are alone requisite to accomplish, sooner or later, the downfal — not of one rite merely — but of the entire fabric of Hindoo superstition. The whole of that system, as has been remarked, stands or falls together; and, though the compulsory abolition of Suttee in our own dominions could do little towards damaging Hindooism, still every such enactment by an independent native state — proceeding, as it does, on a voluntary recognition of the heterodoxy of the rite — assumes necessarily the fallibility of the priesthood, the legitimacy of religious criticism, and, in a word, admits reason into the region of absurdity. This is the great end which abolitionists have ever had in view. On the other hand, the fact is equally certain, that every state which continues to uphold the rite, helps to inspire doubt and distrust in those who have ventured on its abolition. This constitutes the danger of desisting prematurely from our work.

It would be invidious, perhaps, to inquire too closely on whom the responsibility of the stagnation, now visible, rests. Nor is it necessary to ask, why the author of a movement which governors-general have singled out as the chief triumph of their administrations, and for which cabinet-ministers have claimed credit in Parliament, should yet be dwelling amongst us undistinguished by any mark of honour from the Crown. Colonel Ludlow's fame takes no detriment from such neglect, though the public service may. But the graver consideration cannot be omitted, that lethargy in carrying out the measures initiated by that officer, is only too likely to deprive us of the ground already won. In dealing with prejudices which are but partially abated, a passive policy is not even a stationary one — inaction means reaction.

To guard, if it be possible, against so shameful a result, by recalling public attention at home to the subject, is the end sought to be gained by reprinting this little narrative. Englishmen need, perhaps, to be reminded how powerful is any expression of their sympathy in animating the efforts of their distant countrymen. Hitherto our Indian empire has been doomed to interest us chiefly by its wars and disasters. It is regarded when darkened by some sinister eclipse — is watched with anxiety till light is restored — and then is noticed no more than the sun at noon-day. Let us hope that a better era has begun. Britain has now the opportunity of winning an imperishable title to the gratitude of the East. She has but to resolve — and the bloodless contest here recorded will be pursued to issues as far surpassing present calculation, as the results already gained transcend historical experience. But the opportunity is fleeting; let her resolve in time.

Temple, May, 1855.

THE END.